W9-AJT-292

International Food Library

FOOD IN CHINA

International Food Library

FOOD IN CHINA

Jennifer Tan

Rourke Publications, Inc.
Vero Beach, Florida 32964

Library of Congress Cataloging-in-Publication Data

Tan, Jennifer, 1958-
Food in China/by Jennifer Tan.
p. cm. - (International food series)
Includes index.
Summary: Surveys food products, customs, and preparation in China, describing regional dishes, cooking techniques, and recipes for a variety of meals.
ISBN 0-86625-338-6
1. Cookery, Chinese - Juvenile literature. 2. Food habits - China - Juvenile literature. 3. China - Social life and customs - Juvenile literature. [1. Cookery, Chinese. 2. Food habits - China. 3. China - Social life and customs.] I. Title. II. Series.
TX724.5.C5T354 1989
394.1'0951-dc19 88-31644
CIP
AC

CONTENTS

AN INTRODUCTION TO CHINA

China is a vast country that dominates the eastern part of the Asian continent. It covers an area of just over 3.7 million square miles and contains a variety of landscapes, people, and traditions. With a population of over one billion, China is the third largest country in the world. The country is divided into 21 provinces, 3 municipalities, and 5 regions that have some degree of independent government. Among these regions are Tibet and Inner Mongolia.

Chinese culture and history can be traced back to the fifth century B.C., when small communities of farmers cultivated the fertile land to the south of Beijing (also known as Peking). By conquering neighboring lands, the

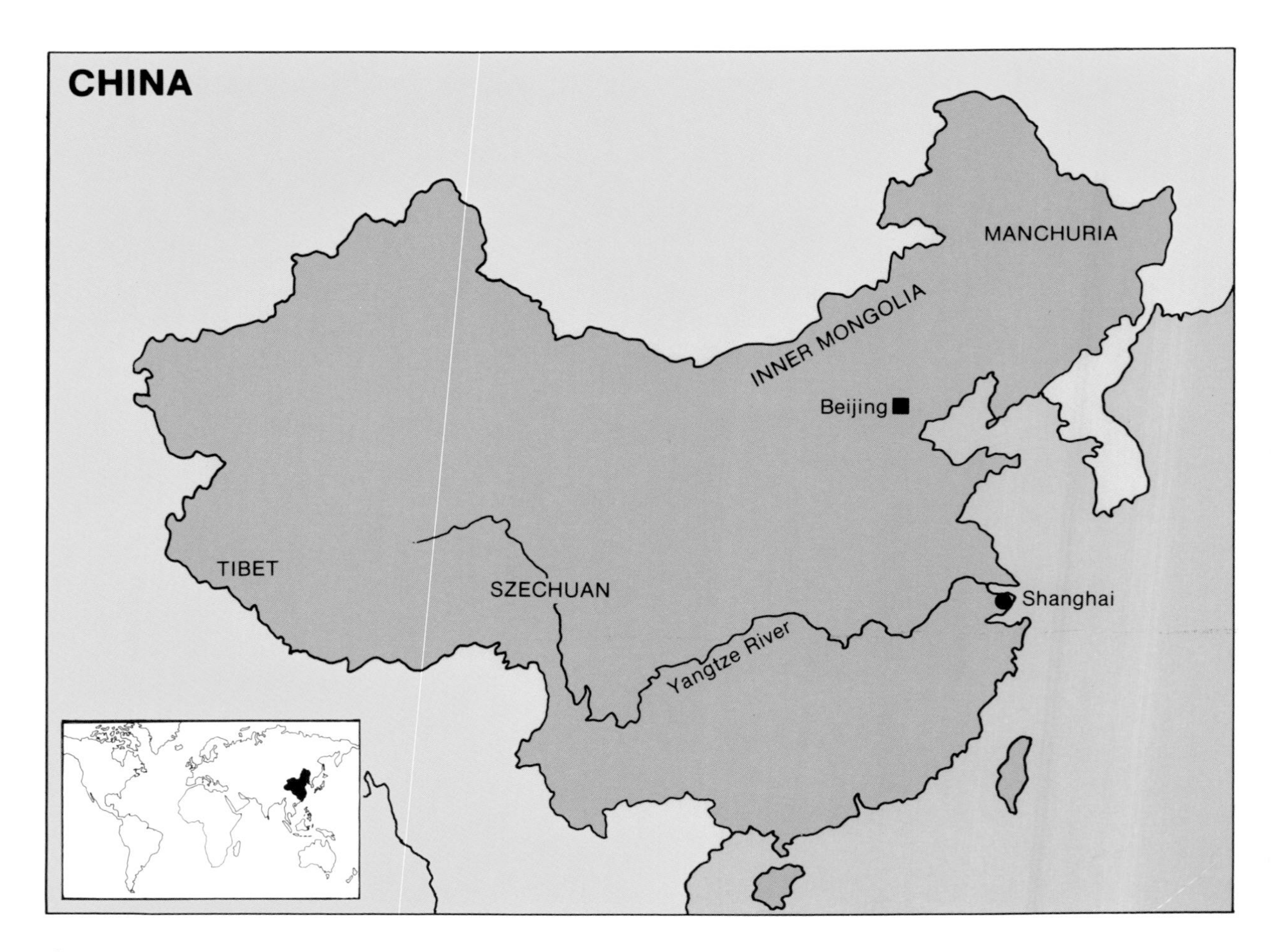

Situated on China's west coast, Shanghai is a major international port and one of China's most important cities.

Chinese spread their influence and administration across a widening area. During the mid-eighteenth century, under the Qing (Manchu) Dynasty, the great Chinese Empire was at its height. It was not to last. The nineteenth century brought civil wars that led to the fall of the Manchu Dynasty and a time of political confusion in the first half of the twentieth century.

In 1949, Mao Zedong led the Chinese people in a communist revolution to establish the People's Republic of China. The infant communist party made many mistakes that hurt China both socially and economically. Today a series of modernization programs is developing China's industrial and agricultural base and providing a more comfortable way of life for the people. Products and services from the western world are welcomed by the Chinese government, which has placed agricultural needs high on its list of requirements. Machinery, livestock, fertilizers, and updated farming techniques are all being imported to China.

AGRICULTURE IN CHINA

The majority of China's 1.1 billion people live in the southern and eastern provinces. The climate there is milder and the land more fertile than in the high mountains of the Tibetan plateau. This inhabited area coincides with the principal agricultural regions; less than one-sixth of China's extensive lands are suitable for farming.

How does China feed her huge population? Three-quarters of the work force, or about 300 million people, work on the land. For years, these people, mostly peasants, worked on collective farms run by the government. China's recent agricultural reforms have changed this system. Families are now free to choose the crops they grow, setting aside an agreed quota to be sold to the government. Any surplus crops may be used or sold by the family that grew them. This so called "responsibility system" of farming is continuously improving agricultural production.

Poultry farming plays an important part in China's agricultural program. Duck farms like this are common throughout China.

Bright green rice plants color the paddies in this collective farm near Canton in southern China.

The staple foods of China are rice and wheat, and these are the most important crops grown. The rice crop has increased by over twenty percent since 1978, and wheat by nearly forty percent. Even so, China has to import over $1.5 billion worth of cereals each year to keep pace with the growing population. In contrast, China is able to export fruit and vegetables to a value of around $1 billion.

China grows a wide variety of food crops, including corn, soybeans, barley, millet, sorghum, oats, potatoes, peanuts, sugar cane, beets, and many different kinds of fruit and vegetables. Livestock such as pigs, sheep, and cattle are generally less important than crops, but the Chinese government is putting new emphasis on poultry farming, particularly duck farming.

FOOD IN CHINA

The Chinese make full use of the many kinds of foods produced in China. Most of the basic foodstuffs — rice, wheat, corn, potatoes, meat, fish, fruit, and vegetables — are well known to us and used in our western cooking. Some of the other, more exotic ingredients are less familiar. Subtle blends of herbs and spices and sauces made from ancient recipes give Chinese food its own particular flavor. Food is chopped into bite-sized pieces and is usually cooked quickly over a hot flame or steamed to retain its flavor and color. These fast-cooking methods are very nutritious, as they preserve the food's natural vitamins.

Most Chinese people shop at the colorful markets, where seasonal fruit and vegetables are piled high on the stalls. Butchers sell pork, beef, and poultry. Those lucky enough to live close to the ocean can buy an astonishing array of seafood and fish.

Chinese people often eat out at roadside foodstalls like this.

Many kinds of foods are available at this street market in southern China.

The Chinese are sociable eaters and often eat out with their family and friends. For lunch, they may snack on rice dumplings stuffed with meat or sweet bean paste or have a filling bowl of rice or noodles with meat and vegetables. In the evening they eat a more substantial meal. This usually consists of several courses; sometimes many dishes are served at the same time and shared by all the diners around the table.

The Chinese eat with chopsticks instead of with a knife and fork. Using chopsticks looks difficult, but with a little practice it soon becomes second nature. A porcelain or plastic spoon is always provided for soups and desserts.

RICE

Rice plays a vital part in the Chinese diet. It is usually boiled in water until the grains swell and become soft and fluffy. Boiled or steamed rice is traditionally served with meat or fish dishes. Rice can be used in many different ways. It is often pounded into flour that is used to make sweet pastries, dumplings, and rice noodles. Rice wine is an alcoholic beverage and is also used to flavor some dishes. Many poor people eat only rice with a little meat or vegetables.

China has been cultivating rice for over five thousand years. Today, most of China's rice is grown in the southern provinces. Much of the rice crop is still grown by hand, although the Chinese are trying to use more machines to increase the crops. The rice fields are first plowed, sometimes using small motorized plows. Then the rice seeds are sown by hand. When the rice seedlings are between 25 and 50 days old, they are transplanted into flooded fields called rice paddies.

Farm workers plant rice seedlings in the paddy fields.

This rice-threshing drum is worked by a treadle, like an old-fashioned sewing machine.

The rice paddies have been thoroughly churned up, the mud softened and ready to accept the young plants. Preparing the paddies is a hard job. The farmer must trudge through the muddy fields, guiding along his water buffalo and the harrow. This is followed by the back-breaking task of planting out the seedlings.

Soon the rice paddies are bright green with the young shoots of growing rice. When the plants are about 130 days old and around two feet tall, they are ready to be harvested. Harvesting is done by hand, and the rice is threshed so that only the rice grains remain. The rice "straw" that is left when the rice has been threshed is used for feeding livestock, thatching roofs, and making mats.

SOYBEANS

Soybeans are one of the world's most nutritious and versatile crops. They are high in proteins similar to those found in meat. Since there is little meat in China, soybeans are of great value in the Chinese diet. The Chinese have cultivated soybeans since the beginning of their civilization, and early records point to their importance. Soybeans were one of the five sacred grains considered essential to the well-being of the Chinese population. The others are rice, wheat, millet, and barley.

Soybeans are a reliable crop. They grow well in most soils, succeeding well in the fertile plains of Manchuria and North China and the lowlands of Szechuan and the Yangtze Valley. With their deep roots, the plants can withstand dry conditions, and some kinds are very resistant to pests. The beans are harvested annually when the plants have reached their full size and the leaves have dropped. Exposed to the sun, the soybeans dry out and can be easily stored.

These soybean plants have been left out to dry in the sun so that the beans can be stored without rotting.

This picture shows bean pods growing on a soybean plant (*Glycina max*).

Soybeans are an important ingredient in Chinese cooking. Sprouts grown from soybean seeds are used in salads and stir-fry recipes. They are rich in Vitamin C and can be grown quickly all year round. Fermented soybeans and parched wheat create the famous soy sauce. This dark brown, salty sauce is a must for all Chinese cooks.

The soybeans themselves are presented in a variety of ways. Boiled in a sweet syrup, they can be used in desserts and cakes. Roasted soybeans taste just like nuts. Soybeans are milled into flour which, mixed with water, produces a delicious milky drink. This mixture can be made into bean curd, or *tofu*, as the Chinese call it. Like soybeans, *tofu* is used in both sweet and savory dishes.

REGIONAL COOKING

Chinese food is as varied as its countryside and its people. Each area uses locally produced foodstuffs, adapting its dishes to suit its climate. Northern recipes call for the use of wheat-based products, while the southern rice-producing provinces rely heavily on rice. Generally, food from the warm south and east of China is lighter than that prepared in the cooler provinces.

Inner Mongolia, Tibet, and other regions that have been annexed by the People's Republic of China retain much of their own culture and tradition. Mongolian food is a little heavier than most Chinese fare, using beef and poultry in larger quantities. The barbecued meat dishes are guaranteed to keep out the cold northern winds.

Cantonese rice dumplings, or dim sum, make a delicious lunchtime snack.

Using a Mongolian firepot, each person cooks his or her own pieces of fish and meat around the table.

Shanghai food from the eastern provinces is lightly spiced and usually cooked in different sauces. Shanghai cooks take advantage of the plentiful seafood in that part of China and produce delicious meals using fish, shrimp, crab, and shark fin.

Szechuan food has recently become popular in the United States. This western Chinese cooking is characterized by its hot, spicy dishes. The liberal use of fiery chilies is thought to keep out the damp mountain air of Szechuan province.

Most Chinese food offered in restaurants in the United States is based on Cantonese recipes from the south of China. Cantonese food is delicate and beautifully presented. It is famous for its pastries and rice dumplings and for its subtle blending of light spices.

THE CHINESE NEW YEAR FESTIVAL

Chinese New Year is the most important event in the Chinese festive calendar. Each new year is seen as the beginning of a new and better time in a person's life and is looked forward to with great excitement.

Shopping for Chinese New Year begins at least one month beforehand. Shoppers comb the markets for traditional items: oranges for good luck, cards to send to their family and friends, and decorations for their homes. Most New Year decorations are red, the traditional lucky color of the Chinese.

Chinese New Year falls in January or February according to our calendar. Each year is characterized by one of twelve animal symbols: horse, rat, pig, rabbit, dragon, snake, ox, tiger, sheep, monkey, rooster, and dog.

Traditionally red, these inscribed Chinese New Year decorations are sold everywhere.

Chinese New Year is also a time for great displays of song and dance. These young girls are waiting for their turn to dance.

Each house is cleaned from top to bottom, and may even be repainted. The old year's cobwebs are swept away. On New Year's Eve, the whole family gathers together at home. Strips of red paper seal the doors to prevent the family's wealth escaping into the night. The family offers prayers to their ancestors before feasting on a huge supper consisting of ten or twelve courses. Later on, at midnight, the paper seals are taken down from the door to let in the good New Year spirits, and the celebrations get under way to a hail of firecrackers.

The Chinese New Year holiday lasts for three days. It is a time for family reunion and for the young members of a family to pay their respects to the older members. At each visit they receive an "Ang Pao," a small red packet inscribed with lucky Chinese symbols containing a present of money.

A BANQUET MENU FOR A FESTIVE OCCASION

Tea Eggs Garnished With Cucumber
Hot And Sour Soup
Baked Fish With Sesame Seed Oil
Mixed Stir-Fried Vegetables
Beef With Oyster Sauce
Boiled Rice
Selection Of Fresh Fruit

Chinese banquets normally have ten to twelve courses. These include hors d'oeuvres, soup, fish and meat dishes, vegetables, and rice served toward the end of the meal. At a banquet, each course is served individually. This festive menu consists of seven courses and is designed for six people. Present the dishes in the above order, serving the rice at the same time as the beef dish.

Tea Eggs Garnished With Cucumber

6 hard-boiled eggs, still in shells
2 teaspoons tea leaves
1 teaspoon sugar
¼ teaspoon salt
1 tablespoon soy sauce
1 cucumber, sliced

1. Roll the hard-boiled eggs gently around a hard surface so that the shells crack all over.
2. Place the eggs in a saucepan with the tea leaves, sugar, salt, soy sauce, and 3¾ cups water. Bring to a boil and simmer gently for one hour. Turn the eggs now and then to be sure they are coloring all over. Leave to cool in the pan.
3. When cool, carefully peel the eggs. They will have a marbled pattern.
4. Arrange the eggs with slices of cucumber.

Hot And Sour Soup.

Hot And Sour Soup

½ cup Chinese mushrooms, finely shredded
½ cup bamboo shoots, finely shredded
½ cup raw ham, finely shredded
4 cups chicken stock
2 tablespoons soy sauce
2 tablespoons wine vinegar
½ teaspoon salt
½ teaspoon white pepper
2 eggs

1. Cook the mushrooms, bamboo shoots and ham in the chicken stock for 3 minutes. Add the soy sauce, vinegar, salt, and pepper and boil gently for 2 minutes.
2. Beat the eggs and stir into the soup. Serve hot.

Baked Fish With Sesame Seed Oil

6 small fish fillets (snapper, sole, or halibut)
¼ cup all-purpose flour
1 teaspoon salt
¼ teaspoon white pepper
2 tablespoons oil
3 tablespoons sesame seed oil

1. Sprinkle the fish fillets with the flour, salt, and pepper.
2. Heat the vegetable oil in a large pan or wok. Gently fry the fish until lightly browned on both sides and place on a serving plate.
3. Heat the sesame seed oil and pour over the fish immediately before serving. Garnish with slices of tomato and spring onion.

Beef With Oyster Sauce

1 lb. flank steak, cut into thin strips
1 teaspoon minced garlic
1 teaspoon sugar
1 teaspoon salt
1 teaspoon cornstarch
2 tablespoons beef stock
2 tablespoons oyster sauce
2 tablespoons oil

1. Sprinkle the beef with salt and cornstarch.
2. Heat the oil in a large pan and fry the garlic for 1 minute. Add the beef and fry lightly until browned.
3. Mix the oyster sauce with the beef stock and sugar and add to the beef in the pan. Cook for 2 minutes and serve hot.

Mixed Stir-Fried Vegetables.

Mixed Stir-Fried Vegetables

½ cup bamboo shoots, finely shredded
1 cup snow peas
1 onion, thinly sliced
½ sweet red pepper, finely shredded
1 stick celery, finely shredded
1 carrot, finely shredded
½ teaspoon sugar
¼ teaspoon salt
1 tablespoon soy sauce
3 tablespoons oil

Heat the oil in a large pan or wok, and fry the onion and garlic for ½ minute. Add the other vegetables and stir-fry for 1 minute. Sprinkle with sugar, salt, and soy sauce. Cook for 1 more minute. Serve hot.

A PEKING STYLE MEAL

Beef With Tomatoes
Crab Omelette
Boiled Rice

These are typical northern-style dishes. Beef is a favorite in the cold winter, while crabs are plentiful during the summer months. Omelettes, or *fu yung*, of all kinds are a regional specialty. You can substitute mushrooms for the crab if you prefer. Serve the beef and omelette dishes together with the boiled rice.

Beef With Tomatoes

½ lb. flank steak
2 large tomatoes
1 tablespoon finely chopped onion
½ cup beef stock
3 tablespoons oil
2 teaspoons soy sauce
1 teaspoon minced garlic
½ teaspoon salt
½ teaspoon sugar
dash of white pepper
2 teaspoons cornstarch

1. Cut the steak into thin strips 2 inches long.
2. Heat 1 tablespoon of oil in a pan and fry the steak for 1 minute. Remove the meat from the pan.
3. Cut each tomato into eight wedge-shaped pieces.
4. Heat the remaining 2 tablespoons of oil in the pan and fry the garlic for 1 minute. Add the tomato, onion, soy sauce, salt, and sugar and stir-fry for ½ minute.
5. Return the steak to the pan and add the stock. Boil for 2 minutes, then add the cornstarch mixed with a little water to thicken the sauce. Serve hot.

Crab Omelette.

Crab Omelette

¼ lb fresh or canned crab meat, shredded
2 scallions, finely chopped
6 eggs
1 teaspoon cornstarch mixed with 2 teaspoons water
¼ teaspoon salt
1 teaspoon soy sauce
¼ teaspoon sugar
2 tablespoons oil

1. Beat the eggs with the cornstarch mixture, salt, and sugar until smooth. Add the crab and scallions to the mixture.
2. Heat the oil in a pan the and stir in the egg mixture. Stir-fry the mixture until it begins to thicken. Fry gently until golden brown. Season with soy sauce and serve hot.

A SZECHUAN STYLE MEAL

Chicken With Dried Red Chilies
Stir-Fried Green Beans With Mushrooms
Boiled Rice

All the dishes in this typically family-style meal should be served at the same time. First make the bean dish and boil the rice. Keep them warm over low heat while preparing the chicken. The hot, spicy chicken dish is balanced by the strong but delicate flavor of the vegetables and rice.

Chicken With Dried Red Chilies

1 lb. chicken breast
1 sweet red pepper
2 dried red chili peppers
¼ onion, chopped
1 teaspoon ginger root, finely chopped
1 teaspoon soy sauce
2 teaspoons wine vinegar
1 teaspoon salt
4 tablespoons oil

1. Cut the chicken breast into 1 inch cubes and add salt.
2. Remove the seeds from the sweet red pepper and cut it into 1 inch strips. Remove the seeds from the dried red chili peppers and chop them into very small pieces.
3. Heat 2 tablespoons of the vegetable oil in a large pan. Add the chicken pieces and stir-fry for 3 minutes. Remove the chicken from the pan and place on an extra plate.
4. Heat the remaining oil in the pan and add the peppers, onion, and ginger. Stir-fry for 1¾ minutes. Add the soy sauce and wine vinegar and stir-fry for ¾ minute. Return the chicken to the pan and stir-fry for 1 more minute. Serve hot, garnished with chopped scallions.

Chicken with dried red chilies.

Stir-Fried Green Beans With Mushrooms

½ lb. green beans
¼ lb. button mushrooms
4 tablespoons oil
1 tablespoon soy sauce
1 teaspoon sugar
1 teaspoon salt
1 cup water

1. Wash the green beans and mushrooms. Cut the larger mushrooms in half.
2. Heat 2 tablespoons of oil in a pan and add the green beans. Stir-fry for 1 minute until the beans have absorbed the hot oil. Add salt and water. Cover and cook until the beans are tender. Remove the beans and remaining water from the pan.
3. Heat 2 more tablespoons of oil in the pan and return the beans and the mushrooms. Add the soy sauce and sugar and stir-fry for 1 minute. Serve hot.

AN EVERYDAY MEAL

Many Chinese people eat a bowl of noodles with meat or fish and vegetables as a light meal. This simple recipe provides a satisfying lunch for four people.

Noodles and rice form the basis of many Chinese meals.

Stir-Fried Pork With Noodles

¼ lb. pork tenderloin
¼ lb. egg noodles
8 snow peas
3 scallions
⅓ cucumber
1 cup bean sprouts
½ teaspoon minced garlic
1 teaspoon salt
2 tablespoons oil

1. Soak the noodles in lukewarm water for 15 minutes. Drain in a colander.
2. Finely shred the pork, snow peas, scallions, and cucumber by cutting in strips lengthwise.
3. Wash the bean sprouts and drain in a colander.
4. Heat the oil in a large pan or wok. Add the shredded pork and minced garlic and stir-fry until lightly browned. Add the drained noodles and stir-fry for 30 seconds. Add the remaining ingredients and stir-fry for 2 minutes. Serve immediately.

GLOSSARY OF COOKING TERMS

For those readers who are less experienced in the kitchen, the following list explains the cooking terms used in this book.

Chopped	Cut into small pieces measuring about ½ inch
Finely chopped	Cut into very small pieces measuring about ⅛ inch
Garnished	Decorated
Minced	Chopped into tiny pieces or put through a mincer
Seeded	Having had the seeds removed
Shredded	Cut into lengths of 1 - 2 inches, about ¼ inch across; shredding can be done with a knife or by rubbing the item against the large holes of a grater
Finely shredded	As above, but about ⅛ inch across
Simmer	The lowest setting on a stove, usually marked
Sliced	Cut into pieces that show part of the original shape of the vegetable
Thinly sliced	As above, but thinner
Spoon measurements	Tablespoons and teaspoons should be filled only to the level of the spoon's edge, not heaped
Stir-fry	To fry quickly in very hot oil while stirring continuously

CHINESE COOKING

To make the recipes in this book, you will need the following equipment and ingredients, which may not be in your kitchen:

Bamboo shoots Canned bamboo shoots are available at most large supermarkets.

Chinese mushrooms These large, dark mushrooms are normally bought dried from a specialty shop and must be soaked in water before use. If they are not readily available, use large mushrooms.

Ginger root Fresh ginger is widely used, and can be bought in small pieces at most supermarkets.

Oil The Chinese prefer peanut or sunflower oil. Olive oil, butter and heavy oils do not allow the natural flavor of the food to come through. Sesame seed oil is required for one of the recipes.

Oyster sauce Bottles of oyster sauce can be bought at some supermarkets and specialty stores.

Soy sauce This salty sauce is an essential in the Chinese kitchen. It can be bought at most supermarkets.

Wok This is a shallow, bowl-shaped pan used to stir-fry.

k and chicken are
rfully coated with
ce and displayed
sale with other
served meats.

INDEX

We would like to thank and acknowledge the following people for the use of their photographs and transparencies:

Anthony Blake Photo Library: 25; Bruce Coleman Ltd: (Hans Gerd Heyer): 7; (Norman Myers): 9; (B & C Alexander): 11; (Michael Viard): 15, (Michael Freeman): 17; Ebury Press: 21, 23; Heather Angel: Cover, T/Page, 12/13, 14; HKTA: 8, 10, 12, 16, 18/19; Octopus Publishing Group—Peter Myers: 27, 28.